MONSTER KNOWS PLEASE and THANK YOU

by Connie Colwell Miller

illustrated by Maira Chiodi

PICTURE WINDOW BOOKS
a capstone imprint

It's Oogle Day! It's time for fun!
Monsters eat and play.

Even though they'll make a mess,
they know the words to say.

Monster gives a friendly knock—

RAP, RAP upon the door.

"PLEASE, my friend, may I come in
and roll on your mud floor?"

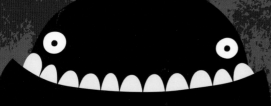

5

Inside the house, a pile of slop

is what the monsters see.

"THANK YOU," says a monster friend, "for inviting me."

The monsters squish
around and slosh
in mud so gooey and brown.

She gulps a cup of sea slug slime.
Soon Monster's tongue turns blue.

"I feel much better," she says to her friend.
And then she says, "THANK YOU."

Oh, no! A monster cannot reach.
The toys are way too high.

He asks his friend, "Will you PLEASE grab
that oozy, stinky fly?"

The tall friend smiles a sharp-toothed grin

and helps the little guy.

"THANK YOU!" says the smaller one,
and soon he flies the fly.

Next it's time to play a game,
a game called Spin-the-Splurn.

There's no grabbing!

Monster asks,

MAY I PLEASE TAKE MY TURN?

Spin-the-Splurn is oogly fun.

The oogliest one wins.

All the monsters say, "THANK YOU."

They all enjoyed the spins.

It's time for one last special treat.

The monsters come when called.

"PLEASE take one home, my friends.

It's eel egg sweets for all!"

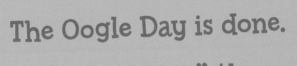

The Oogle Day is done.

"Good-bye," the monsters roar.

"THANK YOU," every monster says.

"Next time, we'll play next door!"

READ MORE

Bently, Peter. *Say Please, Little Bear.* New York: Sandy Creek, 2011.

Dahl, Michael. *Penguin Says Please.* Hello Genius. Mankato, Minn.: Picture Window Books, 2012.

Knapman, Timothy. *The Pirate Who Said Please.* Marvelous Manners. Irvine, Calif.: QEB Pub., 2012.

INTERNET SITES

FactHound offers a safe, fun way to find Internet sites related to this book. All of the sites on FactHound have been researched by our staff.

Here's all you do:

Visit *www.facthound.com*

Type in this code: 9781479522002

 **Super-cool stuff!** Check out projects, games and lots more at **www.capstonekids.com**

Look for all the books in the series:

Thanks to our adviser for his expertise, research, and advice:
Terry Flaherty, PhD, Professor of English
Minnesota State University, Mankato

Editor: Shelly Lyons
Designer: Ashlee Suker
Art Director: Nathan Gassman
Production Specialist: Laura Manthe
The illustrations in this book were created digitally.

Picture Window Books are published by Capstone,
1710 Roe Crest Drive, North Mankato, Minnesota 56003
www.capstonepub.com

Library of Congress Cataloging-in-Publication Data
Cataloging-in-publication information is on file with the Library of Congress.
978-1-4795-2200-2 (library binding)
978-1-4795-2963-6 (board book)
978-1-4795-2951-3 (paperback)
978-1-4795-3326-8 (eBook pdf)
Written by Connie Colwell Miller

Printed in the United States of America in North Mankato, Minnesota.
092013   007772CGS14